## 26 Easy & Adorable

# Alphabet Recipes
# for Snacktime

by Tracy Jarboe and Stefani Sadler

S C H O L A S T I C
**PROFESSIONAL BOOKS**

New York • Toronto • London • Auckland • Sydney
Mexico City • New Delhi • Hong Kong • Buenos Aires

## Dedication

To my Aunt Arline who always made cooking fun! Your creations are forever etched in my mind and heart!  —*Tracy*

For my family who helped me taste-test my culinary creations.  —*Stefani*

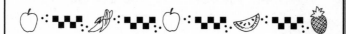

Cover design by Andrew Jenkins

Cover artwork by Shelley Dieterichs

Interior design by Sydney Wright

Interior artwork by Stefani Sadler

ISBN: 0-439-30359-1

Copyright © 2002 by Tracy Jarboe and Stefani Sadler

All rights reserved. Published by Scholastic Inc.

Printed in the U.S.A.

1 2 3 4 5 6 7 8 9 10    40    08 07 06 05 04 03 02 01

# Contents

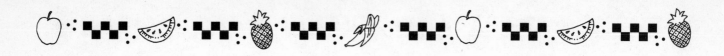

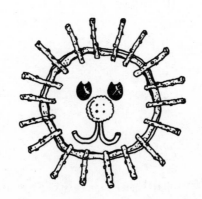

# Introduction

**Welcome** to *26 Easy & Adorable Alphabet Recipes for Snacktime*! You'll soon discover lots of fun and delicious ways to introduce your students to all the letters of the alphabet!

You'll find that these no-cook recipes for fun foods turn ho-hum snacktime into learning time. Each recipe helps your students practice letter sounds and build phonemic awareness. What's more, by following these recipes in your classroom, you'll provide students with hands-on opportunities to develop fine motor skills and to practice measuring and counting. It's learning and fun rolled into one!

Everything you need is here! To help make cooking in your classroom a success, we've included how-to illustrations for quick reference and cross-curricular poems and activities to compliment your favorite themes. Plus, you'll find lots of helpful tips from us—teachers with more than thirty years of combined experience cooking in the classroom.

So put on your apron and push up your sleeves. It's time to make scrumptious snacks . . . from A to Z!

# How to Use This Book

The **26** recipes in this book have been written in an easy step-by-step format and can be readily prepared in the classroom. To set your students on the path to cooking success, model preparation and assembly before you start cooking. Divide your students into small groups or work as a whole class. For older students, you can turn cooking into a learning center activity. Be sure to provide your students with the ingredients, tools, and the recipe with the how-to directions you want them to follow.

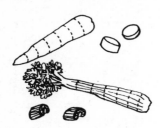

## Each Alphabet Recipe Comes With . . .

### A Poem

Recipe-inspired poems bring meter, rhyme, alliteration, and new vocabulary to your letter lessons. Your students are sure to enjoy reading, chanting, and reciting each playful poem.

### Activities

Take learning the alphabet a step further with cross-curricular extension activities for each letter that invite students to write, predict, dance, and more.

### Book Links

Celebrate every letter of the alphabet with fun-to-read literature. Read the stories aloud. Then tuck them in your classroom library for your students to enjoy.

## Tips

Need to simplify a recipe or find fun ideas for substitutions? Refer to the tips that accompany each recipe. The tips are packed with ideas for making cooking in the classroom quick and easy.

# A Word About Manners

Whether at home, at school, or in a restaurant, table manners are key to a positive dining experience. Help your students develop these important social skills by practicing and role-playing polite table manners. When practiced on a regular basis, table manners help students build confidence, communication skills, and social knowledge. As you help your students determine what polite table manners look like in the classroom, remember to be sensitive to cultural differences.

# Share the ABCs of table manners with your students!

**A** Always wash your hands before eating, and use a napkin to wipe your hands and mouth at the table.

**B** Be considerate of everyone at the table, and wait until each person is seated before eating.

**C** Cheerful conversation and assistance with cleanup are basics of good table manners.

# Tips for Successful Classroom Cooking

## Before you begin . . .

- Make a photocopy of the recipe page. Read the recipe from beginning to end with your students. Examine the illustrated directions together.

- Make sure you have all of the necessary ingredients.

- Store perishable ingredients in a refrigerator or ice chest.

- Cover your work surface with newspaper or butcher paper for easier cleanup.

Wash your hands thoroughly with antibacterial soap and warm water. Have your students do the same.

Protect your clothing with an apron or smock. Invite your students to wear aprons too.

Gather all your ingredients and utensils. Then place them on the work surface in the order that they will be used.

Show your students the utensils they will be using and how to use them.

Let your students know how they can help in the cooking process.

Cut food on a nonporous cutting board, and cut away from you and your students.

Open cans carefully. Dispose of sharp-edged lids promptly.

Invite your students to help, stir, knead, measure the ingredient amounts, and so on.

Talk about the cooking process with your students. Encourage them to share their cooking experiences and questions.

Encourage your students to help clean up any spills.

## After you've finished . . .

Wash all utensils and cooking surfaces thoroughly.

Tuck all clean utensils and ingredients back into their correct storage spaces.

## While you're working . . .

Follow the recipe one step at a time, reading aloud. This a great opportunity for your students to see how adults read and reread directions.

🍎 Share your culinary creations with parents, other teachers, and administrators.

🍎 Store leftovers in airtight containers and refrigerate as needed.

🍎 Invite your students to set the tables and prepare to eat.

🍎 Discuss the experience with your students. Record their ideas on chart paper. Then, send home a letter to parents, sharing some of the cooking highlights and classroom learning.

🍎 Pat yourself on the back. You did a great job!

**Tip!** Invite parents to come and take photos of students in action. Then use the recipes in this book and the photos to make a cooking scrapbook or class recipe book.

## Food Allergy Tips

◆ Make a list of students with food allergies and their emergency contact information on brightly colored paper. Post it where you can easily refer to it—on a refrigerator or cabinet door. In the event of any reaction, seek medical help immediately.

◆ Read all food ingredient labels. Manufacturers occasionally change ingredients in their products.

◆ Keep a list of emergency procedures to follow.

◆ Store emergency medications in a safe, yet handy, location.

◆ Periodically review emergency precautions and school guidelines.

◆ Keep a supply of alternate ingredients available.

◆ Call the Food Allergy Network for information and support at 1-800-929-4040.

# Aa is for Apple-Apricot Kabob

### Poem

## The ABCs

Learning all the ABCs
Start with "A" and end with "Z."
"A" for apple, "B" for blue,
"M" for me and "Y" for you.
Learning all the ABCs
Is how we'll start to
read, read, read!

## Activities

◆ Have students practice making patterns with colored blocks, buttons, or cards marked with "A", "B", and "C". Patterns could include the following:

AABBAABBAABB        ACACACACACAC        ABCABCABCABC

◆ Practice making patterns with other edibles, such as: grapes, raisins, bananas, kiwi fruit, and pineapple.

◆ After eating kabobs, graph which fruit was each student's favorite. Which fruit was the class favorite?

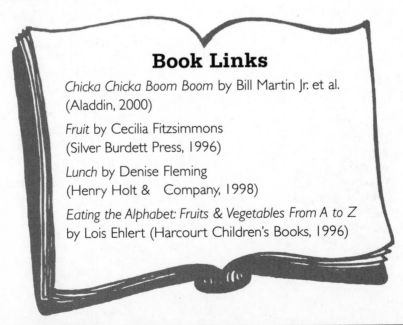

## Book Links

*Chicka Chicka Boom Boom* by Bill Martin Jr. et al.
(Aladdin, 2000)

*Fruit* by Cecilia Fitzsimmons
(Silver Burdett Press, 1996)

*Lunch* by Denise Fleming
(Henry Holt & Company, 1998)

*Eating the Alphabet: Fruits & Vegetables From A to Z*
by Lois Ehlert (Harcourt Children's Books, 1996)

# Aa is for
# Apple-Apricot Kabob

This recipe makes about 8 kabobs.

### Ingredients
1 large apple
6 dried apricots
8-10 wooden skewers

### Utensils
knife
craft sticks
bowl

**1** Wash, core, and slice apple. Cut apple slices into thirds.

**2** Cut apricots into quarters.

**3** Pierce fruit with plastic knife, and place the fruit on the craft stick in ABAB order.

🍎 Young children may do some cutting with a plastic knife and adult supervision.

🍎 For younger students, use craft sticks in place of skewers. Use soft fruit such as bananas and melon.

**TIPS**

⚙ Dipping apples in lemon juice prevents darkening.
⚙ Kabobs rolled in cinnamon sugar or in orange juice and coconut are tasty treats.

# Bb is for Brown Bear Bagel

### Poem

#### Bears

Little bears, big bears,
Howling bears, growling bears,
Lumbering out among the trees,
Stealing honey from the bees.
Watch out! If a bear you see,
When walking out among the trees.

## Activities

◆ Arrange a teddy bear "still life" for your students to sketch or paint. Pose bear with a toy on a chair. Or, pose bear with a lunch box, red apple, and a bear story book.

◆ Compose a class story about a bear using a story starter such as: "On the way to the picnic the bear . . ." Write each story sentence on a different piece of paper and have the children illustrate them. Bind the pages together to make a class book.

◆ Have a teddy bear picnic. Invite each of your students to bring a favorite bear from home to join them as they eat their brown bear bagel.

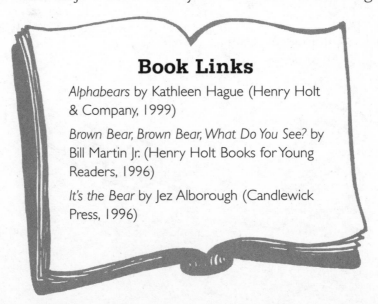

### Book Links

*Alphabears* by Kathleen Hague (Henry Holt & Company, 1999)

*Brown Bear, Brown Bear, What Do You See?* by Bill Martin Jr. (Henry Holt Books for Young Readers, 1996)

*It's the Bear* by Jez Alborough (Candlewick Press, 1996)

# Bb is for
# Brown Bear Bagel

This recipe makes about 20 bears.

## Ingredients

1 pkg. mini-bagels sliced
1 small jar of peanut butter
1 pkg. of crackers
1 pkg. of tiny chocolate morsels

## Utensils

knife

**1** Spread a generous layer of peanut butter on 1/2 of a bagel.

**2** Press 2 crackers in as ears.

**3** Place a cracker over the bagel "hole" to form the nose.

**4** Use chocolate morsels as eyes and a nose. Use additional peanut butter as glue where needed.

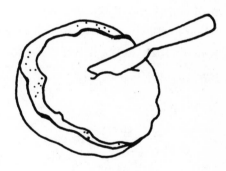

TIPS

○ Try covering each bear with chocolate sprinkles to make fur.

○ Chocolate spreads make a great substitute for peanut butter.

○ Experiment with cereals, chocolate candies, raisins, or nuts to create different types of bears.

# Cc is for Clown Cake

## Poem

### Circus Clowns

Circus clowns have come to town,
They're crazy, cute, and clever.
They do some tricks,
Some jokes, some flips,
I hope they will stay forever!

## Activities

◆ Have a silly clown day. Invite students to wear mismatched, brightly colored clothing. Use jump ropes, Hula-Hoops, and stuffed animals to do circus tricks on the playground.

◆ Make patchwork-collage clowns. Draw a simple outline of a clown and make copies for each student. Have students cut pieces of wrapping paper and glue them onto their clown outline.

◆ Write or dictate to the prompt: "If I were in the circus . . . "

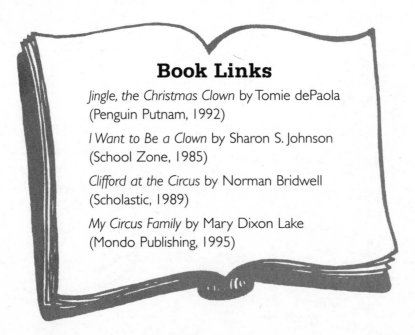

## Book Links

*Jingle, the Christmas Clown* by Tomie dePaola
(Penguin Putnam, 1992)

*I Want to Be a Clown* by Sharon S. Johnson
(School Zone, 1985)

*Clifford at the Circus* by Norman Bridwell
(Scholastic, 1989)

*My Circus Family* by Mary Dixon Lake
(Mondo Publishing, 1995)

# Cc is for Clown Cake

This recipe makes about 12 clown cakes.

## Ingredients
1 pkg. of rice cakes
1 large tub of softened cream cheese
cheese spread in a squeeze dispenser
1 small box of raisins
1 large carrot
1 small jar of pitted cherries

## Utensils
knife      grater      peeler

**1** Wash, peel, and grate carrot.

**2** Slice cherries in half.

**3** Spread cream cheese on top of a rice cake.

**4** Press in carrot shreds for hair, raisins for eyes, halved cherry for a nose. Use the cheese spread to make a mouth.

TIPS

✿ Substitute any of the following for clown hair: shredded cheese, sprouts, coconut, Chinese noodles, etc.

✿ Substitute any of the following for the clown face: grapes, olives, peanuts, carrot slice, etc.

# Dd is for Dinosaur Dig

### ( Poem )

## Dinosaur Days

Imagine how the earth would shake,
When dinos walked around the place.
Their grunts and growls would fill the air,
Their fearsome eyes would squint and stare,
Other creatures would scatter everywhere,
When dinos walked the earth.

## Activities

◆ Have students draw imaginary dinosaurs with crayon, chalk, or pastels. Ask your students to write a description of the dinosaurs. Are they plant or meat eaters? Large or small? Aquatic? Friendly or mean? Challenge your students to come up with names for the dinosaurs, perhaps the "Stefasaurus," "Tracyadon," "Daveadactyl," etc.

◆ Make a class graph of favorite dinosaurs. Which dinosaur is the class favorite?

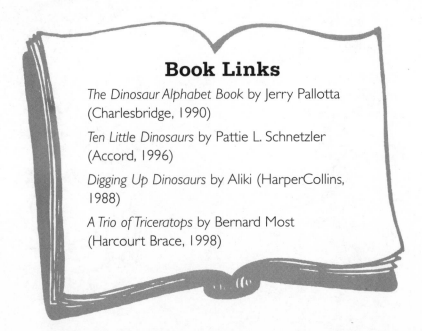

### Book Links

*The Dinosaur Alphabet Book* by Jerry Pallotta
(Charlesbridge, 1990)

*Ten Little Dinosaurs* by Pattie L. Schnetzler
(Accord, 1996)

*Digging Up Dinosaurs* by Aliki (HarperCollins, 1988)

*A Trio of Triceratops* by Bernard Most
(Harcourt Brace, 1998)

# Dd is for Dinosaur Dig

This serves 20 young paleontologists.

## Ingredients

1 box of graham crackers
1 pkg. of chocolate cream-filled cookies
5 four-packs of banana or vanilla pudding
5 four-packs of chocolate pudding
1 large jar of peanuts
1 bag of shredded coconut
1 bottle of green food coloring (optional)
1 dinosaur to hide (A small plastic dinosaur is best, but you can use gummy or cookie dinosaurs with very young children.)

## Utensils

20 clear 16 oz. plastic cups
wire wisk          bowls
rolling pin        resealable bags

**1** Tint coconut green, using a small amount of food coloring and a plastic resealable bag (optional). Set aside.

**2** Crush graham crackers and cookies separately, using a resealable bag and rolling pin.

**3** Make layers as pictured in the illustration, although the order is not important.

TIPS

○ When crushing the graham crackers and cookies, place them in resealable bags. It helps to double the bag before crushing it with a rolling pin. (There should be as little air as possible in the bag before rolling.)

○ Pudding is also available in #10 cans that can be found in any restaurant-supply store.

○ Plastic dinosaurs are usually available at party supply stores and toy stores.

# Ee is for Eggstraterrestrial

### Poem

## Eggs

Eggs in the batter,
Eggs in the pan.
Eggs in my salad,
Eggs with my ham.
Eggs in a basket,
Eggs in a nest.
Eggs in my tummy
Are the eggs I like best!

## Activities

◆ Eat green eggs and ham after reading Dr. Seuss's *Green Eggs and Ham*. Just add a little green food coloring as you beat the eggs. (optional) Then put them in a frying pan and scramble them up!

◆ Make flying saucers (Frisbees). Ask each student to invert a heavy paper bowl or plate and paint it silver. Then have them decorate it with jewels, stickers, and silver pipe cleaners.

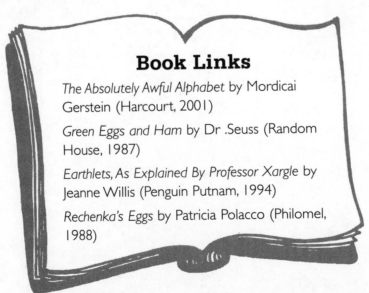

## Book Links

*The Absolutely Awful Alphabet* by Mordicai Gerstein (Harcourt, 2001)

*Green Eggs and Ham* by Dr .Seuss (Random House, 1987)

*Earthlets, As Explained By Professor Xargle* by Jeanne Willis (Penguin Putnam, 1994)

*Rechenka's Eggs* by Patricia Polacco (Philomel, 1988)

# Ee is for Eggstraterrestrial

This recipe makes 24 eggstraterrestrials.

## Ingredients
12 hard-boiled eggs
3 tablespoons of creamy Italian salad dressing
48 thin pretzel sticks
48 mini-marshmallows
24 peanuts
48 olive slices
1 bottle of green food coloring (optional)

## Utensils
knife        fork        bowl
measuring spoons

**1** Peel and halve the hard-cooked eggs. Remove the yolks, put in bowl and mash with a fork.

**2** Add 3 tablespoons of creamy Italian salad dressing to the yolks and stir. Then, add a few drops of food coloring (optional) until the mixture becomes "alien green."

**3** Stuff the egg whites with the yolk mixture.

**4** Place a mini-marshmallow on the end of each pretzel stick. Use two of these to make antennae, and then add 2 olive slice eyes and 1 peanut nose to each egg to complete your eggstraterrestrial!

TIPS

✿ Consider pre-peeling the eggshells for very young children.
✿ Try substitutions for features: shoe-string potato or carrot stick antennae, cereal or cheese nose, etc.

# Ff is for Freshwater Fish

### ( Poem )

## Freshwater Fish

Freshwater fishes,
Swimming in a row.
Gliding in the water,
See how fast they go.
Along comes an alligator,
Looking for his supper.
Little fishes dart away,
Back home to their mother!

## Activities

◆ Have the class make fish prints. Buy several whole fish. Begin by brushing each fish lightly with a dark-colored poster paint. Then, press a sheet of paper onto the fish's surface. Gently rub the entire fish through the paper to form a print.

◆ Make addition or subtraction sentences using fish-shaped crackers as manipulatives. Here is a sample sentence: There were five fish swimming in the stream. Along came a hungry bear who took one fish away. Then there were four fish left ($5 - 1 = 4$). Ask a child to play the hungry bear that eats the fish-shaped cracker.

## Book Links

*The Freshwater Alphabet Book* by Jerry Pallotta (Charlesbridge, 1996)

*The Rainbow Fish* by Marcus Pfister (North-South Books, 1996)

*Swimmy* by Leo Lionni (Alfred A. Knopf Books, 1987)

*From Acorn to Zoo* by Satoshi Kitamura (Scholastic, 1992)

# Ff is for
# Freshwater Fish

This recipe makes 20 crystal blue streams.

### Ingredients
1 bunch of celery
16 oz. of cream cheese
1 box of fish-shaped crackers
blue food coloring (optional)

### Utensils
knives      spoon      bowl

**1** Stir several drops of blue food coloring into the 16 oz. of cream cheese. (optional).

**2** Separate, wash, and cut the celery stalks into 4" sections.

**3** Give each child one 4" celery section and spread a generous amount of the blue cream cheese in the hollow of each celery stalk.

**4** Press 4 fish-shaped crackers into the water (cream cheese) and let the fish swim downstream into your tummy.

🍎 Young children may do some slicing with a plastic knife and adult supervision.

TIPS

✿ The children can mix the cream cheese and food coloring (optional) in a resealable bag for ooshy-gooshy fun.

# Gg is for Graham Garden

## Garden

April showers
Will bring May flowers.
From a seed
They grow with speed.
Soon a garden
And begging your pardon,
Are those weeds?
Well, pull them please!

## Activities

◆ Plant a fruit and vegetable garden. Ask your students to predict what they think will sprout first. Graph the predictions.

◆ Begin a class beautification project! Find an area in the community that needs a little color and plant a rose bush or a flower garden.

◆ Create a window garden. Put an avocado seed, carrot top, or potato in water and watch it grow. Add a different seed or plant each month.

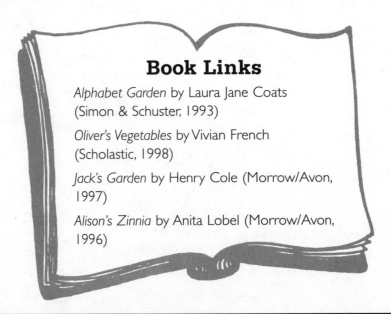

### Book Links

*Alphabet Garden* by Laura Jane Coats (Simon & Schuster, 1993)

*Oliver's Vegetables* by Vivian French (Scholastic, 1998)

*Jack's Garden* by Henry Cole (Morrow/Avon, 1997)

*Alison's Zinnia* by Anita Lobel (Morrow/Avon, 1996)

# Gg is for Graham Garden

This recipe makes 1 delicious garden.

## Ingredients
1 cinnamon graham cracker
honey in a squeeze dispenser
sliced almonds
sesame seeds
1 box of stick pretzels
1 bag of gummy worms
2 teaspoons of peanut butter

## Utensils
knife
measuring spoons

**1** Drop one teaspoon of peanut butter on the top half of the graham cracker.

**2** Form one flower center and sprinkle sesame seeds on it. Place sliced almonds around the edge of the flower center to form petals.

**3** Squeeze a line of honey from the "flower" to stick on the pretzel stem.

**4** Squeeze a line of honey to form the ground and sprinkle sesame seeds on top.

**5** Squeeze a line of honey below the ground to "glue" on the gummy worm.

TIPS

✿ Warm honey (in the window sill or microwave) so it will flow easier.

✿ Green decorator's gel may substitute for honey.

✿ Try toasted coconut for "grass" and a variety of dried fruits or nuts for flowers or trees.

# Hh is for Honey Handwich

Poem

### Hands

Hands for holding.

Hands for shaking.

Hands for giving.

Hands for taking.

Hands for counting one to ten.

Hands for writing with a pen.

Hands are helpful.

Hands are dandy.

But most of all,

Hands are handy!

## Activities

◆ Have each child taste three different types of honey. Clover, orange, and cinnamon are popular flavors. Graph the one that each child liked the best. Which honey is the class favorite?

◆ Make bird feeders by rolling pinecones in honey or peanut butter and then in birdseed. Hang them on a tree and let the birds enjoy!

## Book Links

*Love is a Handful of Honey* by Giles Andreae (ME Media, 2001)

*A Honey of a Day* by Janet Perry Marshall (HarperCollins, 2000)

*Sam's Sandwich* by David Pelham (Random House, 1990)

*Clap Your Hands* by Lorinda Bryan Cauley (Penguin Putnam, 2001)

# Hh is for
# Honey Handwich

### Ingredients
1 large slice of bread
1 teaspoon of honey
1 teaspoon of butter

### Utensils
knife
hand-shaped cookie cutter
bowl

**1** Place honey and butter in a small bowl and mix with a spoon until smooth.

**2** Place the handprint cookie cutter on top of the bread, press through, and peel away excess bread. (Or, using a plastic knife, cut around a child's hand.)

**3** Spread honey-butter onto the palm of the hand and now you have a honey handwich!

- Try using flavored honey for a different twist.
- Stir cinnamon into the mixture for a extra-yummy treat!
- Feed birds with bread scraps.

# Ii is for Icy Cream

**Poem**

## Ice Cream

I like to shiver,
I like to shake.
I like ice cream
With my cake,
And with my cookies,
And with this rhyme.
Oh, I like ice cream all the time!

## Activities

◆ Make paper snowflakes and then write about the snowflakes' adventures. Ask your students: Did the snowflakes become a snowman, an igloo, a ski run? Where did they fall and what did they see before melting away?

◆ Make icy paints by filling the bottom half of an ice cube tray with tempera paints and the top half with water. Let the paints freeze and then let the children paint using the ice. (Craft sticks can be inserted before freezing if you prefer.) It takes a few minutes for the ice cubes to melt down enough to really give vibrant color, but be patient and you'll be delighted by the results!

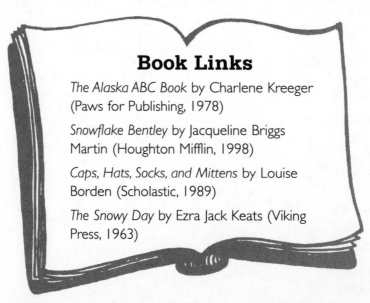

### Book Links

*The Alaska ABC Book* by Charlene Kreeger (Paws for Publishing, 1978)

*Snowflake Bentley* by Jacqueline Briggs Martin (Houghton Mifflin, 1998)

*Caps, Hats, Socks, and Mittens* by Louise Borden (Scholastic, 1989)

*The Snowy Day* by Ezra Jack Keats (Viking Press, 1963)

# Ii is for
# Icy Cream

This makes 2 servings of icy cream.

## Ingredients

1 cup of milk
1/2 teaspoon of vanilla
2 tablespoons of sugar
12 tablespoons of salt
a tray of ice
gallon- and quart-size resealable freezer bags

## Utensils

cup measure
measuring spoons
bowl

**1** Place the ice and salt inside the gallon bag and place all other ingredients into the quart-size bag. Seal the quart-size bag after squeezing all the air out of it.

**2** Place the smaller bag inside the larger bag containing the ice and salt, and seal it.

**3** Shake back and forth for about 5 minutes, until the mixture thickens.

**4** Eat directly from the bag or pour into a bowl. Enjoy!

TIPS

❖ Before eating the icy cream out of the bag, be sure to quickly rinse the smaller bag in cold water to eliminate all the salt.

❖ Try adding sprinkles, nuts, color, etc.

# Jj is for Jungle Juice

( **Poem** )

## Jungle

Deep in the jungle
Swinging on a vine,
Chatting with a parrot
To see what's on his mind,
Strolling with a tiger,
Slithering with a snake,
A visit to the jungle
Is one I have to take!

## Activities

◆ Play jungle animal action games: invite students to walk like a panther, swing like a monkey, slither like a snake, etc.

◆ Make a jungle alphabet book. Have each child draw a different animal for each letter of the alphabet. An accordion fold book works nicely. For example: Aa—alligator, Bb—bear, Cc—crocodile, and so on.

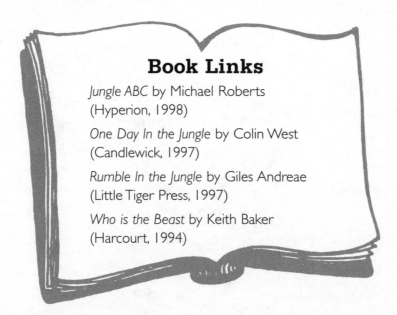

### Book Links

*Jungle ABC* by Michael Roberts
(Hyperion, 1998)

*One Day In the Jungle* by Colin West
(Candlewick, 1997)

*Rumble In the Jungle* by Giles Andreae
(Little Tiger Press, 1997)

*Who is the Beast* by Keith Baker
(Harcourt, 1994)

# Jj is for Jungle Juice

This recipe makes about 12–20 jungle juices, depending upon glass size.

### Ingredients

lemon gelatin
lime gelatin
lemonade

### Utensils

fork    straws    bowl
tall, clear cups or glasses

**1** Flake each gelatin separately in a bowl with a fork.

**2** Layer the gelatin in a cup as shown in the diagram.

**3** Add juice or punch to fill the glass.

**4** Drink and enjoy!

**TIPS**

- Garnish with a mint sprig and a paper umbrella for a tropical effect.
- Garnish with red vine licorice for a swinging touch!
- For extra sparkle, substitute lemon-lime soda for the lemonade.

# Kk is for Kooky Kite

### Kite

It's flying high,
In a bright blue sky.
Dancing around,
Without a sound.
Ribboned tail,
Just watch it sail.
Colors so bright.
What is it?
My kite!

## Activities

◆ Make construction paper kites to display on classroom windows. Try using cellophane or tissue for a more transparent look.

◆ Ask students to write to the prompt: "Where do lost kites go?"

◆ Learn and sing the song, "Let's Go Fly A Kite" from *Mary Poppins*. Then go fly a kite on the playground!

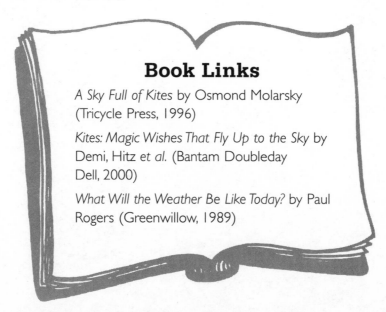

### Book Links

*A Sky Full of Kites* by Osmond Molarsky (Tricycle Press, 1996)

*Kites: Magic Wishes That Fly Up to the Sky* by Demi, Hitz *et al.* (Bantam Doubleday Dell, 2000)

*What Will the Weather Be Like Today?* by Paul Rogers (Greenwillow, 1989)

# Kk is for Kooky Kite

This recipe makes 1 high-flying kite sandwich.

### Ingredients
2 slices of bread
1 slice of bologna or turkey
1 pat of butter
cheese spread in a squeeze dispenser
1 three-inch piece of shoestring licorice

### Utensils
knives

**1** Spread butter on one side of a slice of bread, and top with bologna and the other slice of bread.

**2** Cut off the crust to form a diamond shape.

**3** Squeeze cheese on top to make kite crosspieces.

**4** Place a licorice tail on the back and fly the kite into your mouth!

🍎 Young children may do some slicing with a plastic knife and adult supervision.

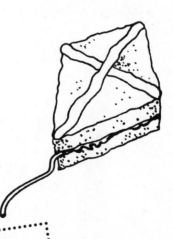

TIPS

⚙ You may use American cheese sliced into strips for the kite crosspieces.
⚙ Decorate the kite with other treats, such as: nuts, olives, ketchup designs, etc.

# Ll is for Lazy Lion

## Poem

### Lazy Lion

There was once a lazy lion
Who slept the day away.
"Get up!" the pride was cryin'.
He smiled and said, "No way!"
"But we can't catch lunch without you,"
The pride began to yell.
"You must get up and help us too!"
But off to sleep he fell.

## Activities

◆ Ask your students to write to the prompt: "If I were King of the Jungle, I would . . ."

◆ Have a "Lazy Day". Invite your students to wear pajamas to school. Spend the day reading animal books and eating popcorn. Be as lazy as you can!

◆ Compare and contrast what the world would be like if everyone was lazy and what the world would be like if no one was lazy.

### Book Links

*A Bold Carnivore: An Alphabet of Predators* by Consie Powell (Roberts Rinehart, 1997)

*ABC Animal Riddles* by Susan Joyce (Peel Productions, 1998)

*Tops and Bottoms* by Janet Stevens (Spoken Arts, 2001)

*Leo the Late Bloomer* by Robert Kraus (HarperCollins, 1998)

# Ll is for
# Lazy Lion

This recipe makes 1 lazy lion.

## Ingredients

1 small flour tortilla
1 small jar of peanut butter
20 small stick pretzels
1 black olive, pitted and
sliced in half
1 butter cracker
2 two-inch pieces of red
shoestring licorice

## Utensils

knife

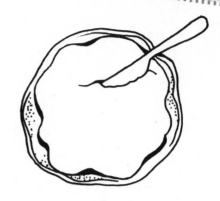

**1** Spread peanut butter on the tortilla to cover it completely.

**2** Press pretzel sticks into peanut butter around the outside edge of the tortilla.

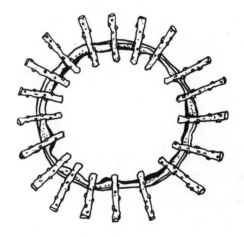

**3** Decorate as follows: use the olive halves for eyes, the butter cracker for a nose, and the licorice for a mouth.

**4** Have a roaring good time eating your lazy lion!

TIPS

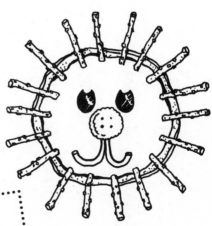

○ Substitute shoestring potatoes for pretzels to form the mane.
○ Substitute round bread or bagel halves for tortillas.

# Mm is for Mocha Monkey Malt

> **Poem**
>
> ## Monkeys
>
> Monkeys in the jungle,
> Monkeys in the zoo.
> Monkeys making mischief,
> Monkeys, "Shame on you!"
> Please don't pick the flowers.
> Please don't spill the glue.
> Monkeys, silly monkeys,
> What shall we do with you?!

## Activities

◆ Read the "Curious George" books and then ask your students to write to the prompt: "I'm curious about . . ."

◆ Play "Monkey See, Monkey Do" by pantomiming an action and having the children copy it.

◆ Read *Caps For Sale* and then dramatize the story using real caps and a large tabletop for the tree. Watch out for falling caps!

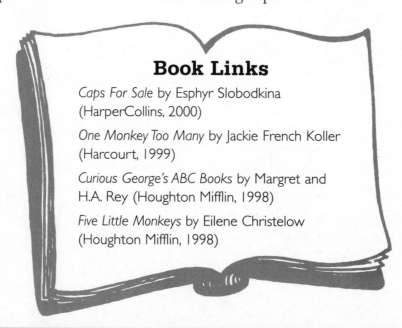

### Book Links

*Caps For Sale* by Esphyr Slobodkina (HarperCollins, 2000)

*One Monkey Too Many* by Jackie French Koller (Harcourt, 1999)

*Curious George's ABC Books* by Margret and H.A. Rey (Houghton Mifflin, 1998)

*Five Little Monkeys* by Eilene Christelow (Houghton Mifflin, 1998)

# Mm is for
# Mocha Monkey Malt

This recipe makes 1 swinging malt!

## Ingredients

1/2 cup of milk
1 generous scoop of
mocha ice cream
1 small banana
1 tablespoon of chocolate
malt syrup

## Utensils

resealable plastic bag
knife          glass

**1** Place the banana in a resealable bag and mash it thoroughly by squeezing.

**2** Add the ice cream and malt syrup, then squeeze until blended.

**3** Add in 1/2 cup of milk and gently squeeze until blended. (This mixture will be lumpy.) Be sure to hold the resealable portion of the bag with one hand and squeeze with the other.

**4** Pour the mixture into a glass or use a straw to sip it out of the bag!

**TIPS**

⚙ Try banana ice cream.
⚙ Soften the ice cream slightly before mixing.

# Nn is for Nifty Necklace

( **Poem** )

## Necklace

My necklace is awesome,
My necklace is neat.
I've created a pattern
Of good things to eat.
O-shaped cereal and candy sweet
I'll wear it all day for a tasty treat.

## Activities

◆ Make name necklaces. Stamp, write, stencil, or print letters with a computer. Cut, laminate, punch holes, and lace.

◆ Make salt dough beads around a plastic straw. When they have dried, paint, coat with clear acrylic, and string.

Salt Dough: Combine 3 cups of flour, 3 cups of salt, and 2 1/4 cups of water. Slowly stir to bread dough consistency and use immediately. Dry beads for 48 hours.

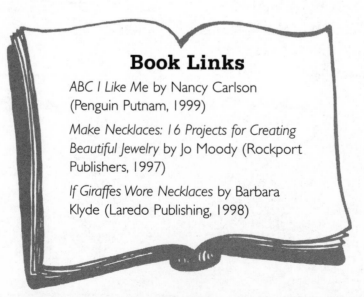

## Book Links

*ABC I Like Me* by Nancy Carlson (Penguin Putnam, 1999)

*Make Necklaces: 16 Projects for Creating Beautiful Jewelry* by Jo Moody (Rockport Publishers, 1997)

*If Giraffes Wore Necklaces* by Barbara Klyde (Laredo Publishing, 1998)

# Nn is for
# Nifty Necklace

**Quantity depends upon number of licorice strings.**

### Ingredients

1 large bag of shoestring licorice
any of the following:
O-shaped cereals,
small pretzels,
O-shaped candies, etc.

### Utensils

wax paper          bowls

**1** Set out bowls filled with a variety of stringable treats.

**2** Have each child create a pattern on a sheet of waxed paper or a paper towel. Check to make sure pattern is correct.

**3** Tie a large knot on one end of a 24" licorice string. Let the children string their patterns.

**4** Tie ends together, wear, and nibble as needed.

TIPS

✿ Tie the knot 2–3 times to securely fasten.
✿ Limit pattern choices for younger children.
✿ On a length of cardboard or construction paper, glue a sample pattern to copy.

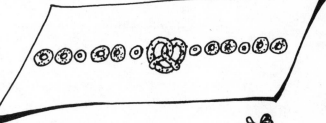

# Oo is for OO-pples and Boo-noo-noos

## Poem

### Oo-pples & Boo-noo-noos

Oo-pples are crunchy.
Boo-noo-noos are sweet.
I think they're munchy
And yummy to eat!

Slice them and dice them,
In bowls or on plates.
Fruit is so healthy.
And sure tastes great!

## Activities

◆ Have an apple tasting party. Prepare or purchase a variety of foods made with apples or apple flavoring. Have an appley good time!

◆ Create fruit prints using apples and bananas. Dip fruit into poster paint and press on paper making different designs and patterns. Try slicing the fruit in a variety of ways and combining colors for interesting effects.

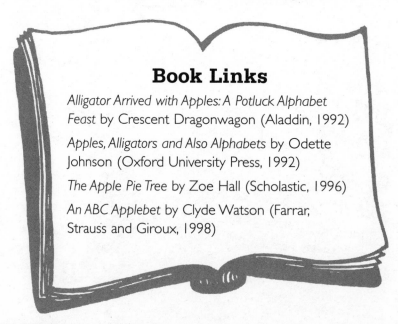

### Book Links

*Alligator Arrived with Apples: A Potluck Alphabet Feast* by Crescent Dragonwagon (Aladdin, 1992)

*Apples, Alligators and Also Alphabets* by Odette Johnson (Oxford University Press, 1992)

*The Apple Pie Tree* by Zoe Hall (Scholastic, 1996)

*An ABC Applebet* by Clyde Watson (Farrar, Strauss and Giroux, 1998)

# Oo is for
# OO-pples and Boo-noo-noos

This recipe makes about 20 oo-pples & boo-noo-noos.

## Ingredients

5 apples
10 bananas
colored miniature marshmallows
1 jar of peanut butter
1 cup of o-shaped cereal
vanilla wafers
miniature peanut butter cups
1 small box of raisins

## Utensils

knives          apple corer

**1** Wash, core, and slice apples crossways, making circles.

**2** Peel and slice bananas into four-inch slices.

**3** Spread some peanut butter on one end of a banana slice. Stand the banana up on the center of one apple slice.

**4** Decorate as follows: raisin eyes, marshmallow nose, carved out mouth, cereal ears, and a vanilla wafer hat with an inverted peanut butter cup on top. Use peanut butter glue as needed.

**TIPS**

○ Dipping the fruit in lemon juice will prevent darkening.

○ Make a small indentation in the banana before "gluing" on the eyes, nose, ears, and mouth.

# Pp is for Peanut-Butter Dough Pretzel

### Poem

## Pretzel Time

Peanut butter is sticky.
Peanut butter is sweet.
Its dough is cool,
And always a treat.
Roll the dough,
Make a snake,
Twist a pretzel,
Mmmm, tastes great!

## Activities

◆ Invite your students to use a variety of pretzels in different shapes and sizes to create pretzel pictures. Glue the pretzels down once the creation is complete.

◆ Predict how many shapes pretzels come in, using as many adjectives as you can to describe your predictions. Purchase the different varieties from the store and make a chart to record your findings. Graph by size, weight, favorite shape, etc.

◆ Build a pretzel town using stick pretzels for logs and peanut butter or royal icing for mortar.

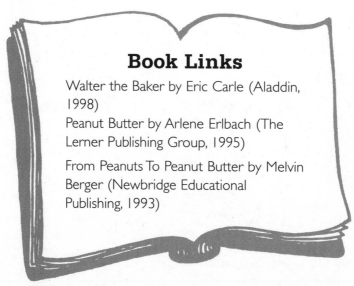

## Book Links

Walter the Baker by Eric Carle (Aladdin, 1998)

Peanut Butter by Arlene Erlbach (The Lerner Publishing Group, 1995)

From Peanuts To Peanut Butter by Melvin Berger (Newbridge Educational Publishing, 1993)

# Pp is for
# Peanut-Butter Dough Pretzel

This recipe makes about 10 pretzels.

### Ingredients
2 cups of non-fat dry milk
1 cup of peanut butter
2 tablespoons of honey

### Utensils
resealable bag
measuring spoons
measuring cups
wax paper

**1** Place all ingredients in a resealable bag.

**2** Knead the ingredients together in the bag.

**3** Give each child a small handful of dough to roll out on wax paper like a snake.

**4** Twist the snake to form a pretzel. Eat!

TIPS

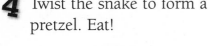
○ Make sure to remove excess air from the resealable bag before kneading dough.
○ Try a variety of sprinkles on the pretzel, such as: cinnamon sugar, toasted coconut, and ground nuts.

# Qq is for Queen of Hearts Cherry Tarts

### Poem

## Queen of Hearts

The Queen of Hearts
Bakes tasty tarts
Of blueberry, cherry, and quince.
She places them on a silver tray
And serves them to the Prince.

The prince bows down,
And smiles wide,
And says thank you to the queen.
"These tarts are very tasty,
And the loveliest I have seen."

## Activities

◆ Have a royal "tea party" and serve tarts from a silver tray. Have the class dress up nicely and play the music of Mozart, Bach, or Handel. Use proper etiquette, such as: bowing, curtsying, using napkins, etc.

◆ Share readings of King & Queen poetry and rhymes such as: Old King Cole.

◆ Have students make tagboard crowns and decorate them with plastic jewels.

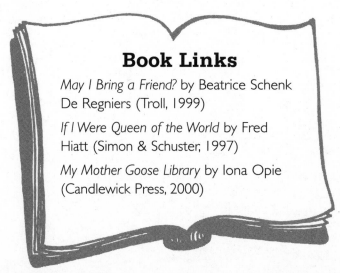

## Book Links

*May I Bring a Friend?* by Beatrice Schenk De Regniers (Troll, 1999)

*If I Were Queen of the World* by Fred Hiatt (Simon & Schuster, 1997)

*My Mother Goose Library* by Iona Opie (Candlewick Press, 2000)

# Qq is for
# Queen of Hearts Cherry Tarts

This recipe makes 16–20 cherry tarts.

## Ingredients

1 box of graham crackers
1 can of cherry pie filling
1 tub of soft margarine
8 individual serving packages of
vanilla pudding

## Utensils

resealable bag     rolling pin
muffin cups        spoons

**1** Place one box of graham crackers in a resealable bag and crush.

**2** Add margarine and knead mixture in the resealable bag.

**3** Place a heaping spoonful of the graham cracker mixture into a muffin cup, followed by a heaping spoonful of vanilla pudding and then a heaping spoonful of cherry pie filling.

**4** Use a spoon to eat this royal treat!

**TIPS**

✿ Make sure to remove excess air from the resealable bag before rolling and kneading dough.

✿ Try tasty variations like blueberry or apple.

# Rr is for Rabbit Refresher

### Poem

## Rabbits

Crunching on some carrots,
Munching on some sprouts.
Rabbits in my garden
Are scurrying about.

Their tails are white and fluffy,
Their noses sniff and twitch.
I wonder how their mothers
Can tell which one is which?

## Activities

◆ Invite the class to sing and dance the "Bunny Hop" around the classroom.

◆ Brainstorm a list of rabbit characters, such as White Rabbit, Bugs Bunny, Rabbit (Pooh), Peter Cottontail, etc. Then read or write about your favorite character.

◆ Create bunny ear hats out of construction paper. Use white cotton or pink fur for the inside of each ear.

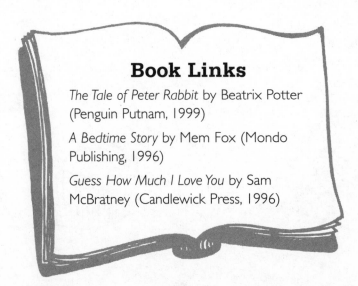

## Book Links

*The Tale of Peter Rabbit* by Beatrix Potter (Penguin Putnam, 1999)

*A Bedtime Story* by Mem Fox (Mondo Publishing, 1996)

*Guess How Much I Love You* by Sam McBratney (Candlewick Press, 1996)

# Rr is for
# Rabbit Refresher

**This hoppingly good snack serves 1.**

### Ingredients

1 pear half (canned)
1 cherry half
6 blanched almonds
1 tablespoon of cottage cheese
1 leaf of iceberg lettuce
1 or 2 carrot sticks

### Utensils

paper towels
measuring spoons

**1** Drain pear half. Wash and dry the lettuce.

**2** Set pear with pitted side down on lettuce.

**3** Place a cherry at the small end for a nose, add almond ears and feet, make raisin eyes, and add a dollop of cottage cheese for a tail.

**4** Add carrot sticks for your rabbit to crunch on.

**TIPS**

✿ Try dipping a marshmallow in juice or water, then rolling it in coconut for the tail.

✿ A grape substitutes nicely for the nose.

45

# Ss is for Silly Spider

> ## Poem
>
> ### Spiders
>
> Creeping, crawling in the dark
> In dusty, musty places,
> Spiders spin their silken webs
> Then hide in secret spaces.
>
> Mother spider spins and spins
> A case to protect her young.
> At last the tiny spiders hatch
> And crawl out one by one.

## Activities

◆ Sing the song, "The Ants Go Marching," but substitute spiders for ants.

◆ Dramatize the story "There Was An Old Lady Who Swallowed A Fly."

◆ Create spider hats by attaching 8 accordion-folded black strips of construction paper to a wide, black construction paper band. Add large googlie eyes, a pom-pom nose, and red crayon mouth.

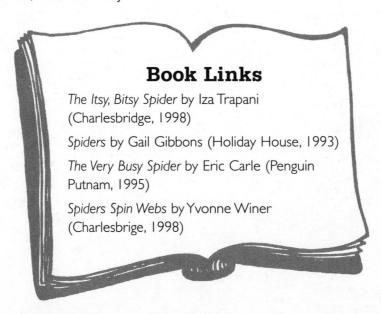

## Book Links

*The Itsy, Bitsy Spider* by Iza Trapani (Charlesbridge, 1998)

*Spiders* by Gail Gibbons (Holiday House, 1993)

*The Very Busy Spider* by Eric Carle (Penguin Putnam, 1995)

*Spiders Spin Webs* by Yvonne Winer (Charlesbrige, 1998)

# Ss is for Silly Spider

**This recipe makes 1 silly spider.**

### Ingredients
1 donut
8 three-inch pieces of shoestring licorice
2 red hots
1 candy corn

### Utensils
none

**1** Push the eight licorice pieces into the donut, placing four on each side.

**2** Push the two red candies onto the front of the donut to make eyes and insert the candy corn (pointed side in) to make a nose.

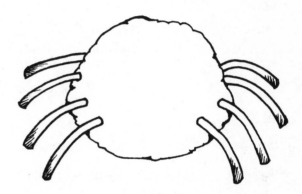

**3** Enjoy your silly spider snack.

**TIPS**

- Use toasted coconut marshmallows for a smaller spider body.
- Make a salad spider with 1/2 tomato body, olive eyes, bean sprout or carrot stick legs, and a raisin nose.
- Make a party spider by using an inverted cupcake or muffin for the spider body.

# Tt is for Toad Taco

## Toads

Toads are spotted,
Toads have bumps.
Toads are timid,
Toads can jump.
Toads hide in hollows,
And wait for bugs.
Toads snack on crickets,
Worms and slugs.

## Activities

◆ Invite your students to research the answer to the question: What are the differences between frogs and toads?

◆ Make pet rock toads. Glue two flat, smooth stones on top of each other. Paint the stones, and glue on googlie eyes. Eyes may also be made from lima beans. These toads make great math manipulatives.

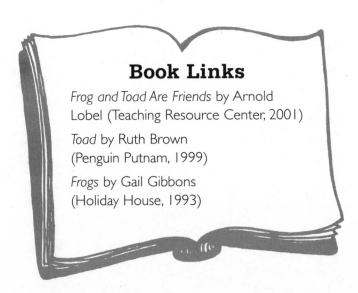

### Book Links

*Frog and Toad Are Friends* by Arnold Lobel (Teaching Resource Center, 2001)

*Toad* by Ruth Brown (Penguin Putnam, 1999)

*Frogs* by Gail Gibbons (Holiday House, 1993)

# Tt is for Toad Taco

This recipe makes 1 tantalizing toad.

## Ingredients

1 taco shell
2 olive slices
1/8 cup of sour cream
1/4 cup of refried beans
1/4 cup of shredded cheese
1/4 cup of shredded lettuce
1 carrot curl
1 raisin

## Utensils

measuring cups
spoon        knife

**1** Put refried beans, then cheese, then lettuce into the taco shell.

**2** Place two small dollops of sour cream on the top edge of the taco shell, and place the two olive slices on the sour cream to make the eyes.

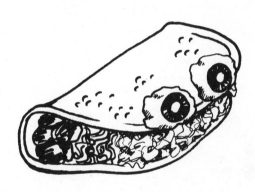

**3** Place the carrot curl in the taco opening with a raisin on the end to form the toad's tongue.

**4** Hop that toad into your mouth!

TIPS

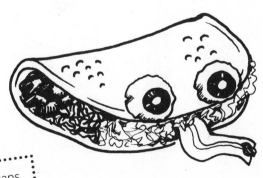

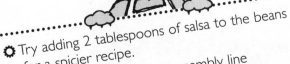

○ Try adding 2 tablespoons of salsa to the beans for a spicier recipe.

○ This recipe lends itself to assembly line construction. Spoon in beans, then cheese, etc.

# U u is for the U.S. Flag

**Poem**

## Hurray for the U.S.A.

I love the U.S.A.
And my flag red, white, and blue.
Here I will always stay,
My heart forever true!

I will stand and say the pledge,
My hand upon my heart.
I love the land of the brave and free.
I want to do my part.

## Activities

◆ Design a class flag and discuss the significance of flags and allegiance.

◆ Make U.S. flag hand-prints. Have each student paint a blue square on the bottom of his or her palm, and paint fingers red and white. Turn the hand over and press it onto white construction paper. Use a cotton swab to add white paint stars. Let it dry and then cut it out and display!

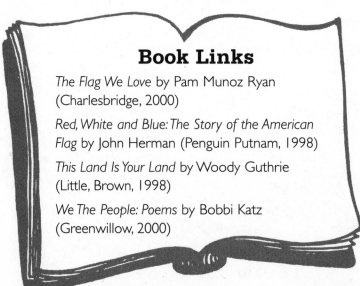

## Book Links

*The Flag We Love* by Pam Munoz Ryan (Charlesbridge, 2000)

*Red, White and Blue: The Story of the American Flag* by John Herman (Penguin Putnam, 1998)

*This Land Is Your Land* by Woody Guthrie (Little, Brown, 1998)

*We The People: Poems* by Bobbi Katz (Greenwillow, 2000)

# Uu is for the U.S. Flag

**This recipe makes 1 U.S. flag.**

### Ingredients
1 graham cracker
1/8 cup of white icing
2 red licorice strips, trimmed to fit
blue decorator icing in a tube
white decorator icing in a tube
with a star tip (or star
shaped sprinkles)

### Utensils
measuring cups        knife

**1** Spread a generous amount of frosting on the graham cracker.

**2** Using blue decorator frosting, paint a square at the top left of the graham cracker. Then make stars with the star-tipped icing tube on the blue square (or place white star sprinkles).

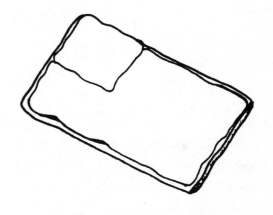

**3** Place trimmed red licorice strips on the graham cracker to make stripes.

**4** Have a Yankee Doodle good time!

TIPS

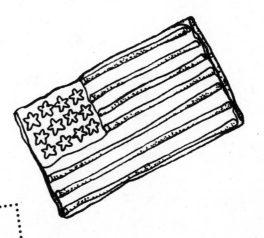

○ Flags may also be made on a toaster pastry.
○ Make a flag cake using white rectangle cake, white icing, blueberry stars, and raspberry stripes.

# Vv is for Veggie Viper

## Venomous Viper

I saw a venomous viper,
Who slithered all around.
He wiggled right onto my plate,
Without making a single sound.

His stripes were made of carrots,
His tomato head so red.
My vegetable viper isn't so vile,
But a tasty treat instead!

## Activities

◆ Write a silly snake poem using as much "s" alliteration as possible.

◆ Make egg carton snakes. Cut an empty egg carton in half. Ask each student to paint the egg carton using vibrant colors. Then have them add a red pipe cleaner tongue and wiggle eyes, too!

◆ Ask students to form a snake conga line and dance, or play "Follow the Leader."

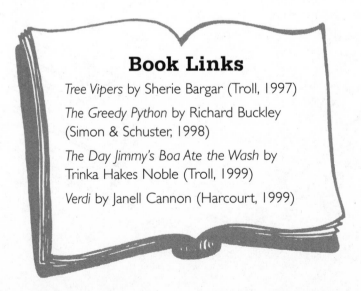

## Book Links

*Tree Vipers* by Sherie Bargar (Troll, 1997)

*The Greedy Python* by Richard Buckley (Simon & Schuster, 1998)

*The Day Jimmy's Boa Ate the Wash* by Trinka Hakes Noble (Troll, 1999)

*Verdi* by Janell Cannon (Harcourt, 1999)

# Vv is for
# Veggie Viper

This recipe makes 1 veggie viper.

### Ingredients
1 large carrot
1 large stalk of celery
1 cherry tomato
1 large piece of lettuce
1 tub of cream cheese

### Utensils
knife

**1** Cut the carrot and celery into 1-inch slices.

**2** Use a large piece of lettuce as a plate.

**3** Spread a small amount of cream cheese on each vegetable slice, then place them side-by-side in a long, coiled row to form a snake.

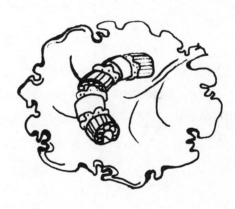

**4** Use the cherry tomato as the head, and cut a forked tongue out of a carrot slice.

**TIPS**

- Try using zucchini, jicama, or radishes for a variation.
- Make sure the vegetables are very dry before you begin.
- Use flavored cream cheese.

# Ww is for Wishing Wand

Poem

## Wishing Wand

If I had a wishing wand
I'd wave it around and say,
Wonderful, wise, and witty words,
Wishing all my worries away.

I might wish for a whistle,
Or maybe a wagon too.
Whatever I happen to wish for,
I want to share it with you!

## Activities

◆ Make up some "magic words" in the style of "abracadabra" and assign them special meanings, such as: when you hear "abbazabba" it is time to clean up.

◆ Plan a magical party. As a class, research magic tricks at the library. Go see a magic show or invite a magician to the party.

◆ Read a story about magic while wearing a cape and top hat.

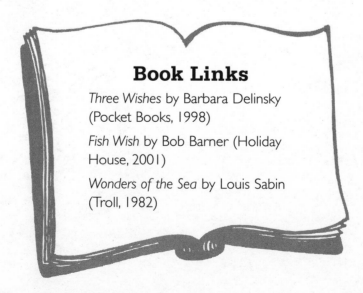

## Book Links

*Three Wishes* by Barbara Delinsky (Pocket Books, 1998)

*Fish Wish* by Bob Barner (Holiday House, 2001)

*Wonders of the Sea* by Louis Sabin (Troll, 1982)

# Ww is for Wishing Wand

This recipe makes 1 magical wishing wand.

## Ingredients

1 large pretzel stick
1 small jar of peanut butter
1/8 cup of chopped nuts

## Utensils

waxed paper
knife

**1** Dip the end of the pretzel stick into peanut butter and coat well.

**2** Roll the peanut butter end in chopped nuts, which have been placed on waxed paper.

**3** Make a wish with your wand and enjoy!

**TIPS**

✿ Instead of peanut butter, try using cream cheese, chocolate frosting, etc.

✿ Instead of nuts, try using sprinkles, sesame seeds, or mini chocolate chips.

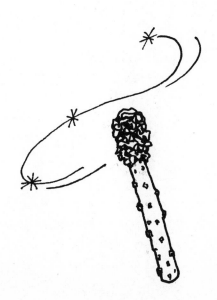

# Xx is for Xs and Os

### Poem

## Xs and Os

Xs neatly in a row
With Os slipped in between.
This message is very special,
Hugs and Kisses is what it means.

I'll write it on the cards I send
And on my letters too.
Don't be surprised if you find
They've all been sent to you!

## Activities

◆ Play Giant Tic-Tac-Toe. Use tape to make a grid on the floor, tongue depressors or craft sticks glued in the center for Xs, and plastic coffee can lids for Os.

◆ Ask students to brainstorm all the words they know that have the letter X in them.

◆ Draw self-portraits. Ask students to make a border around the pictures using Xs and Os. Invite students to give the portraits to someone they love.

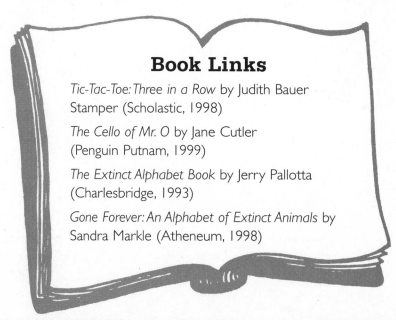

## Book Links

*Tic-Tac-Toe: Three in a Row* by Judith Bauer Stamper (Scholastic, 1998)

*The Cello of Mr. O* by Jane Cutler (Penguin Putnam, 1999)

*The Extinct Alphabet Book* by Jerry Pallotta (Charlesbridge, 1993)

*Gone Forever: An Alphabet of Extinct Animals* by Sandra Markle (Atheneum, 1998)

# Xx is for Xs and Os

This recipe makes 20 hugs and kisses.

**Ingredients**
20 square-shaped crackers
20 slices of American cheese
20 olives

**Utensils**
knife

**1** Cut each slice of cheese into strips and then slice each olive.

**2** Place the cheese strips across the square-shaped cracker to form an X. Put the olive slices on in any order.

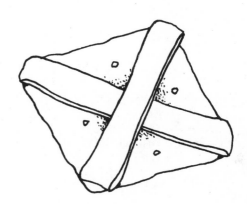

**3** Tic-tac-toe, enjoy your Xs and Os.

TIPS

✿ Put nine crackers together to make a tic-tac-toe board.

✿ Try using crackers spread with peanut butter or cheese spread, and use o-shaped cereals for the Os and pretzel sticks for the Xs.

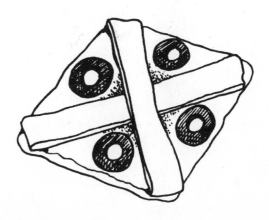

# Yy is for Yo-yo Yummy

### Poem

## Yo-yos

Yo-yos go up,
Yo-yos go down.
Yo-yos even go
Round and round.
Yo-yos go fast,
Yo-yos go slow,
But without me,
My yo-yo won't go.

## Activities

◆ Have a yo-yo share day. Use a yo-yo and demonstrate tricks you have learned.

◆ Discuss what things go up and what things go down. Make a list: rocket, space shuttle, fireworks, submarine, rain, etc.

◆ Yo-yos go up and down. Other things do too. Have your students pretend they are going up in a hot air balloon. Where will we come down? What will we see? Write about the adventure.

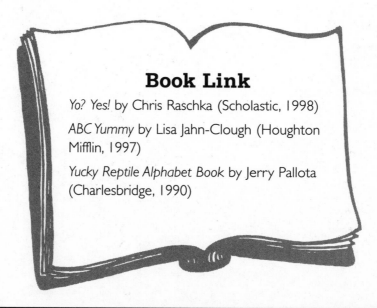

## Book Link

*Yo? Yes!* by Chris Raschka (Scholastic, 1998)

*ABC Yummy* by Lisa Jahn-Clough (Houghton Mifflin, 1997)

*Yucky Reptile Alphabet Book* by Jerry Pallota (Charlesbridge, 1990)

# Yy is for
# Yo-yo Yummy

This recipe makes about 24 yo-yo yummies.

### Ingredients
1 box of round crackers
1 jar of peanut butter
1 or 2 bags of shoestring licorice

### Utensils
knife

**1** Spread a generous amount of peanut butter on a cracker.

**2** Top with another cracker.

**3** Wrap a licorice string around the cracker sandwich to make a yo-yo.

TIPS

✿ Try serving your yo-yo yummy with other yo-yo treats, such as: cucumber slices and cream cheese, or round sandwich yo-yos.

# Zz is for Zany Zoo

## Zoo

I can't spell "elephant" or "cockatoo."
I can't spell "koala" or "kangaroo."
But I know where to find them:
In the z-o-o zoo!

## Activities

◆ Paint a zoo mural on butcher paper with moats, cages, ponds, etc. Ask your students to draw, color, and cut out their favorite zoo animal to add to the mural.

◆ Take a field trip to a zoo!

◆ Invite your students to draw pictures of exotic animals. Hang the pictures side by side to make a picture zoo.

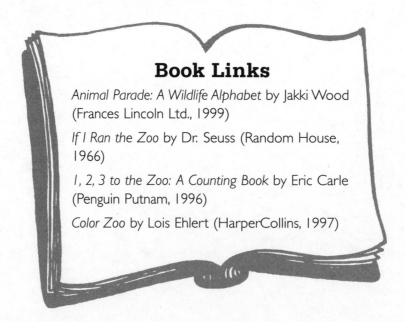

### Book Links

*Animal Parade: A Wildlife Alphabet* by Jakki Wood (Frances Lincoln Ltd., 1999)

*If I Ran the Zoo* by Dr. Seuss (Random House, 1966)

*1, 2, 3 to the Zoo: A Counting Book* by Eric Carle (Penguin Putnam, 1996)

*Color Zoo* by Lois Ehlert (HarperCollins, 1997)

# Zz is for Zany Zoo

### Ingredients

20 graham crackers or small pieces of toast

1 can of white frosting

1 can of white frosting mixed with blue food coloring (optional)

1 cup of coconut mixed with green food coloring (optional)

1 box of animal crackers

1 jar of green decorator sugar crystals

### Utensils

knives

**1** Spread white frosting on each cracker.

**2** Use green coconut and sprinkles to make grass.

**3** Use blue frosting to make rivers and lakes.

**4** Place several animal crackers in your zoo.

**TIPS**

✿ Use a generous amount of frosting to ensure that the animals stand up easily.

✿ Try using gummy animal shapes.

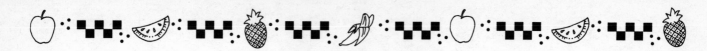

# Recipes

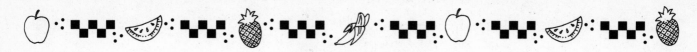

# Recipes

# Recipes